This Book Belongs To :

_____

Index

Name	Page

MY PET INFORMATION

NAME:

BREED:

WEIGHT:

BIRTHDAY: /   /

ADOPTION DATE: /   /

GENDER: MALE   FEMALE   SPAYED/NEUTERED: YES   NO

COAT COLOR: LICENSE#:

EYE COLOR: MICROCHIP#:

SPECIAL MARKINGS: INSURANCE#:

ID CHIP #:   REGISTERED WITH:

MEDICAL INFORMATION

ALLERGIES:

MEDICAL CONDITIONS:

ADDITIONAL INFO   NOTES

FAVORITE TOYS:

FAVORITE TREAT:

VET INFORMATION

NAME/BUSINESS:

PHONE:

EMAIL:

ADDRESS:

NOTES:

GROOMER INFORMATION

NAME/BUSINESS:

PHONE:

EMAIL:

ADDRESS:

NOTES:

PET SITTER INFORMATION

NAME/BUSINESS:

PHONE:

EMAIL:

ADDRESS:

TRAINER INFORMATION

NAME/BUSINESS:

PHONE:

EMAIL:

ADDRESS:

ANIMAL POISON CONTROL

PHONE:

ADDRESS:

NOTES

PET SITTER CHECKLIST

RESPONSIBILITIES	M	T	W	T	F	S	S

TRAINING CHECKLIST

BASIC

- COME
- NO
- SIT
- DOWN
- WATCH ME
- STAY
- ROLL OVER
- SHAKE
- FETCH
- TOUCH
- WAIT
- OK
- SPIN
- HEEL
- TAKE IT
- DROP IT
- OUT
- QUIET
- STAND
- CRAWL
- OFF
- PLACE
- BED
- SETTLE
- GO (TO A PLACE)
- CATCH
- HIGH FIVE
- SPEAK
- BACK
- BANG/PLAY DEAD

ADVANTED

- GO (TO A PLACE)
- FIND IT
- LIGHTS
- LEAP
- PUT TOYS AWAY
- JUMP INTO YOUR ARMS
- FREEZE
- LOOK LEFT
- LOOK RIGHT
- TRACK A PERSON (BY SCENT)
- JUMP THROUGH A HOOP

SOCIALIZATION CHECKLISTS 1

KINDS OF PEOPLE

WOMEN

MEN

TALL/BIG MEN

CHILDREN

TODDLERS CRAWLING

BABIES

PEOPLE WITH MASKS

MEN WITH BEARDS

RUNNERS

PEOPLE WITH SUNGLASSES

PEOPLE IN HATS/HELMETS

PEOPLE WITH HOODS

PEOPLE WITH UMBRELLAS

PEOPLE WITH BIKES

PEOPLE WITH SCOOTERS

PEOPLE WITH SKATEBOARDS

PEOPLE WITH STROLLERS

PEOPLE WITH ROLLERBLADES

PEOPLE WITH TOOLS

PEOPLE WITH WAGONS

PEOPLE IN WHEELCHAIRS

PEOPLE WITH CANES/WALKERS

ANIMALS

PUPPIES

DOGS-FEMALE

DOGS-MALE

BIG DOGS

LITTLE DOGS

CATS

KITTENS

BIRDS

DUCKS/GEESE

SQUIRRELS

RODENTS

SHEEP

CHICKENS

HORSES

CATTLE

DEER

PLACES

VET

CAR

STORES

PLAYGROUND

PARK/DOG PARK

BEACH

STAIRS

ELEVATOR

CROWDED PLACES

OTHER PEOPLES HOUSES

LAKE

STREAM

POOL

SCHOOLS

HIKING TRAILS

BOATS

KAYAKS/CANOES

RAILWAY CROSSING

SPORTS FIELDS

TUNNELS

BRIDGES

SOCIALIZATION CHECKLISTS 2

SURFACES

- HARDWOOD
- TILE/STONE FLOOR
- WOOD
- METAL
- SAND
- SNOW
- PAVEMENT
- ROCKS
- LEAVES
- GRASS
- SNOW/ICE
- SLICK FLOORS
- CARPET
- WATER/PUDDLES
- MUD
- LINOLEUM
- REFLECTIVE SURFACES

TOUCH/HANDLING

- PUTTING ON COLLAR/HARNESS
- BEING ON LEASH
- TOUCH/CLEAN EARS
- PAWS (HOLD, GENTLE SQUEEZE)
- NAIL CLIPPING
- TEETH CHECK/ BRUSH
- CLEANING EYES
- BRUSHING COAT
- BATHING

SOUNDS

- CLAPPING
- SINGING
- SHOUTING
- MOTORCYCLE
- SIRENS
- CARS
- MOTORBIKES
- TRACTORS
- TV
- MUSIC
- BARKING DOGS
- DOORBELL
- DISHWASHER
- VACUUM
- LAWNMOWER
- FIREWORKS
- GUNSHOTS
- THUNDER
- ALARM CLOCK

OBJECTS

- TOYS
- BALLOONS
- SKATEBOARDS
- FEATHERS
- TRASH CANS
- AGILITY OBSTACLES
- CLOTHES
- WHEELCHAIRS
- SQUEAKERS
- FANS
- BAGS
- IRON BOARD
- SHOVELS
- BROOMS
- PAPER

SUPPLIES CHECKLIST

HOME

    ID TAG

    COLLAR

    BED

    CRATE

    CRATE PAD

    EXERCISE PEN

    BABY GATE

    PUPPY PADS

    GRASS TRAINING PATCH

    STAIN AND ODOR REMOVER

FEEDING/HEALTH

    FOOD

    FOOD AND WATER BOWL

    DOG FOOD CONTAINER

    TREATS FOR TRAINING

TRAVELING

GROOMING

    BRUSH

    SHAMPOO

    NAIL TRIMMERS

    TOOTHBRUSH

    TOWEL

    PAW BALM

    GROOMING WIPES

TOYS

    CHEW TOY

    DOG PUZZLE TOY

    TUG TOY

    FETCH TOY (BALL/DISC)

    SQUEAKY TOY

MY PET EXPENSES $

MONTH: YEAR:

PET NAME:

EXPENSE TRACKER

DATE	FOOD	VET	MEDICATION	GROOMING	COST
					$
					$
					$
					$
					$
					$
					$
					$
					$
					$
					$
					$
					$
					$
					$
					$
					$
					$
					$
					$
					$
					$
					$
					$
					$
					$
					$
					$
					$

MY PET EXPENSES $

MONTH: YEAR:

PET NAME:

EXPENSE TRACKER

DATE	FOOD	VET	MEDICATION	GROOMING	COST
					$
					$
					$
					$
					$
					$
					$
					$
					$
					$
					$
					$
					$
					$
					$
					$
					$
					$
					$
					$
					$
					$
					$
					$
					$
					$
					$
					$

MY PET EXPENSES $

MONTH: YEAR:

PET NAME:

EXPENSE TRACKER

DATE	FOOD	VET	MEDICATION	GROOMING	COST
					$
					$
					$
					$
					$
					$
					$
					$
					$
					$
					$
					$
					$
					$
					$
					$
					$
					$
					$
					$
					$
					$
					$
					$
					$
					$

MY PET EXPENSES $

MONTH: _____ YEAR: _____

PET NAME: _____

EXPENSE TRACKER

DATE	FOOD	VET	MEDICATION	GROOMING	COST
					$
					$
					$
					$
					$
					$
					$
					$
					$
					$
					$
					$
					$
					$
					$
					$
					$
					$
					$
					$
					$
					$
					$
					$
					$
					$
					$

MY PET EXPENSES $

MONTH: YEAR:

PET NAME:

EXPENSE TRACKER

DATE	FOOD	VET	MEDICATION	GROOMING	COST
					$
					$
					$
					$
					$
					$
					$
					$
					$
					$
					$
					$
					$
					$
					$
					$
					$
					$
					$
					$
					$
					$
					$
					$
					$
					$
					$
					$

MY PET EXPENSES $

MONTH: YEAR:

PET NAME:

EXPENSE TRACKER

DATE	FOOD	VET	MEDICATION	GROOMING	COST
					$
					$
					$
					$
					$
					$
					$
					$
					$
					$
					$
					$
					$
					$
					$
					$
					$
					$
					$
					$
					$
					$
					$
					$
					$
					$
					$

MY PET EXPENSES | | | $

MONTH: YEAR:

PET NAME:

EXPENSE TRACKER

DATE	FOOD	VET	MEDICATION	GROOMING	COST
					$
					$
					$
					$
					$
					$
					$
					$
					$
					$
					$
					$
					$
					$
					$
					$
					$
					$
					$
					$
					$
					$
					$
					$
					$
					$

MY PET EXPENSES $

MONTH: YEAR:

PET NAME:

EXPENSE TRACKER

DATE	FOOD	VET	MEDICATION	GROOMING	COST
					$
					$
					$
					$
					$
					$
					$
					$
					$
					$
					$
					$
					$
					$
					$
					$
					$
					$
					$
					$
					$
					$
					$
					$
					$
					$
					$
					$

MY PET EXPENSES			$

MONTH: YEAR:

PET NAME:

EXPENSE TRACKER		

DATE	FOOD	VET	MEDICATION	GROOMING	COST
					$
					$
					$
					$
					$
					$
					$
					$
					$
					$
					$
					$
					$
					$
					$
					$
					$
					$
					$
					$
					$
					$
					$
					$
					$
					$
					$
					$
					$

MY PET EXPENSES $

MONTH: YEAR:

PET NAME:

EXPENSE TRACKER

DATE	FOOD	VET	MEDICATION	GROOMING	COST
					$
					$
					$
					$
					$
					$
					$
					$
					$
					$
					$
					$
					$
					$
					$
					$
					$
					$
					$
					$
					$
					$
					$
					$
					$
					$
					$
					$

MY PET EXPENSES $

MONTH: YEAR:

PET NAME:

EXPENSE TRACKER

DATE	FOOD	VET	MEDICATION	GROOMING	COST
					$
					$
					$
					$
					$
					$
					$
					$
					$
					$
					$
					$
					$
					$
					$
					$
					$
					$
					$
					$
					$
					$
					$
					$
					$
					$
					$
					$

MY PET EXPENSES $

MONTH: YEAR:

PET NAME:

EXPENSE TRACKER

DATE	FOOD	VET	MEDICATION	GROOMING	COST
					$
					$
					$
					$
					$
					$
					$
					$
					$
					$
					$
					$
					$
					$
					$
					$
					$
					$
					$
					$
					$
					$
					$
					$
					$
					$
					$

VET APPOINTMENT ✚

DATE & TIME: /   /   .   :   AM/PM   CHECK UP: YES   NO

CLINIC: COST:

REASON:

OUTCOME:

FOLLOW UP: YES   NO

FOLLOW UP DATE: /   /   .   :   AM/PM

DATE & TIME: /   /   .   :   AM/PM   CHECK UP: YES   NO

CLINIC: COST:

REASON:

OUTCOME:

FOLLOW UP: YES   NO

FOLLOW UP DATE: /   /   .   :   AM/PM

DATE & TIME: /   /   .   :   AM/PM   CHECK UP: YES   NO

CLINIC: COST:

REASON:

OUTCOME:

FOLLOW UP: YES   NO

FOLLOW UP DATE: /   /   .   :   AM/PM

DATE & TIME: /   /   .   :   AM/PM   CHECK UP: YES   NO

CLINIC: COST:

REASON:

OUTCOME:

FOLLOW UP: YES   NO

FOLLOW UP DATE: /   /   .   :   AM/PM

DATE & TIME: /   /   .   :   AM/PM   CHECK UP: YES   NO

CLINIC: COST:

REASON:

OUTCOME:

FOLLOW UP: YES   NO

FOLLOW UP DATE: /   /   .   :   AM/PM

VET APPOINTMENT ✚

DATE & TIME: / / . : AM/PM   CHECK UP: YES NO
CLINIC: COST:
REASON:
OUTCOME:
FOLLOW UP: YES NO
FOLLOW UP DATE: / / . : AM/PM

DATE & TIME: / / . : AM/PM   CHECK UP: YES NO
CLINIC: COST:
REASON:
OUTCOME:
FOLLOW UP: YES NO
FOLLOW UP DATE: / / . : AM/PM

DATE & TIME: / / . : AM/PM   CHECK UP: YES NO
CLINIC: COST:
REASON:
OUTCOME:
FOLLOW UP: YES NO
FOLLOW UP DATE: / / . : AM/PM

DATE & TIME: / / . : AM/PM   CHECK UP: YES NO
CLINIC: COST:
REASON:
OUTCOME:
FOLLOW UP: YES NO
FOLLOW UP DATE: / / . : AM/PM

DATE & TIME: / / . : AM/PM   CHECK UP: YES NO
CLINIC: COST:
REASON:
OUTCOME:
FOLLOW UP: YES NO
FOLLOW UP DATE: / / . : AM/PM

VET APPOINTMENT   ✚

DATE & TIME: /   /   .   :   AM/PM   CHECK UP: YES   NO
CLINIC: COST:
REASON:
OUTCOME:
FOLLOW UP: YES   NO
FOLLOW UP DATE: /   /   .   :   AM/PM

DATE & TIME: /   /   .   :   AM/PM   CHECK UP: YES   NO
CLINIC: COST:
REASON:
OUTCOME:
FOLLOW UP: YES   NO
FOLLOW UP DATE: /   /   .   :   AM/PM

DATE & TIME: /   /   .   :   AM/PM   CHECK UP: YES   NO
CLINIC: COST:
REASON:
OUTCOME:
FOLLOW UP: YES   NO
FOLLOW UP DATE: /   /   .   :   AM/PM

DATE & TIME: /   /   .   :   AM/PM   CHECK UP: YES   NO
CLINIC: COST:
REASON:
OUTCOME:
FOLLOW UP: YES   NO
FOLLOW UP DATE: /   /   .   :   AM/PM

DATE & TIME: /   /   .   :   AM/PM   CHECK UP: YES   NO
CLINIC: COST:
REASON:
OUTCOME:
FOLLOW UP: YES   NO
FOLLOW UP DATE: /   /   .   :   AM/PM

VET APPOINTMENT

DATE & TIME: /   /   .   :   AM/PM   CHECK UP: YES   NO

CLINIC: COST:

REASON:

OUTCOME:

FOLLOW UP: YES   NO

FOLLOW UP DATE: /   /   .   :   AM/PM

DATE & TIME: /   /   .   :   AM/PM   CHECK UP: YES   NO

CLINIC: COST:

REASON:

OUTCOME:

FOLLOW UP: YES   NO

FOLLOW UP DATE: /   /   .   :   AM/PM

DATE & TIME: /   /   .   :   AM/PM   CHECK UP: YES   NO

CLINIC: COST:

REASON:

OUTCOME:

FOLLOW UP: YES   NO

FOLLOW UP DATE: /   /   .   :   AM/PM

DATE & TIME: /   /   .   :   AM/PM   CHECK UP: YES   NO

CLINIC: COST:

REASON:

OUTCOME:

FOLLOW UP: YES   NO

FOLLOW UP DATE: /   /   .   :   AM/PM

DATE & TIME: /   /   .   :   AM/PM   CHECK UP: YES   NO

CLINIC: COST:

REASON:

OUTCOME:

FOLLOW UP: YES   NO

FOLLOW UP DATE: /   /   .   :   AM/PM

VET APPOINTMENT ✚

DATE & TIME: /   /   .   :   AM/PM   CHECK UP: YES   NO
CLINIC: COST:
REASON:
OUTCOME:
FOLLOW UP: YES   NO
FOLLOW UP DATE: /   /   .   :   AM/PM

DATE & TIME: /   /   .   :   AM/PM   CHECK UP: YES   NO
CLINIC: COST:
REASON:
OUTCOME:
FOLLOW UP: YES   NO
FOLLOW UP DATE: /   /   .   :   AM/PM

DATE & TIME: /   /   .   :   AM/PM   CHECK UP: YES   NO
CLINIC: COST:
REASON:
OUTCOME:
FOLLOW UP: YES   NO
FOLLOW UP DATE: /   /   .   :   AM/PM

DATE & TIME: /   /   .   :   AM/PM   CHECK UP: YES   NO
CLINIC: COST:
REASON:
OUTCOME:
FOLLOW UP: YES   NO
FOLLOW UP DATE: /   /   .   :   AM/PM

DATE & TIME: /   /   .   :   AM/PM   CHECK UP: YES   NO
CLINIC: COST:
REASON:
OUTCOME:
FOLLOW UP: YES   NO
FOLLOW UP DATE: /   /   .   :   AM/PM

VET APPOINTMENT ✚

DATE & TIME: /   /   .   :   AM/PM   CHECK UP: YES   NO
CLINIC: COST:
REASON:
OUTCOME:
FOLLOW UP: YES   NO
FOLLOW UP DATE: /   /   .   :   AM/PM

DATE & TIME: /   /   .   :   AM/PM   CHECK UP: YES   NO
CLINIC: COST:
REASON:
OUTCOME:
FOLLOW UP: YES   NO
FOLLOW UP DATE: /   /   .   :   AM/PM

DATE & TIME: /   /   .   :   AM/PM   CHECK UP: YES   NO
CLINIC: COST:
REASON:
OUTCOME:
FOLLOW UP: YES   NO
FOLLOW UP DATE: /   /   .   :   AM/PM

DATE & TIME: /   /   .   :   AM/PM   CHECK UP: YES   NO
CLINIC: COST:
REASON:
OUTCOME:
FOLLOW UP: YES   NO
FOLLOW UP DATE: /   /   .   :   AM/PM

DATE & TIME: /   /   .   :   AM/PM   CHECK UP: YES   NO
CLINIC: COST:
REASON:
OUTCOME:
FOLLOW UP: YES   NO
FOLLOW UP DATE: /   /   .   :   AM/PM

VET APPOINTMENT

DATE & TIME: /   /   .   :   AM/PM   CHECK UP: YES   NO

CLINIC: COST:

REASON:

OUTCOME:

FOLLOW UP: YES   NO

FOLLOW UP DATE: /   /   .   :   AM/PM

DATE & TIME: /   /   .   :   AM/PM   CHECK UP: YES   NO

CLINIC: COST:

REASON:

OUTCOME:

FOLLOW UP: YES   NO

FOLLOW UP DATE: /   /   .   :   AM/PM

DATE & TIME: /   /   .   :   AM/PM   CHECK UP: YES   NO

CLINIC: COST:

REASON:

OUTCOME:

FOLLOW UP: YES   NO

FOLLOW UP DATE: /   /   .   :   AM/PM

DATE & TIME: /   /   .   :   AM/PM   CHECK UP: YES   NO

CLINIC: COST:

REASON:

OUTCOME:

FOLLOW UP: YES   NO

FOLLOW UP DATE: /   /   .   :   AM/PM

DATE & TIME: /   /   .   :   AM/PM   CHECK UP: YES   NO

CLINIC: COST:

REASON:

OUTCOME:

FOLLOW UP: YES   NO

FOLLOW UP DATE: /   /   .   :   AM/PM

VET APPOINTMENT ✚

DATE & TIME: /   /   .   :   AM/PM   CHECK UP: YES   NO
CLINIC: COST:
REASON:
OUTCOME:
FOLLOW UP: YES   NO
FOLLOW UP DATE: /   /   .   :   AM/PM

DATE & TIME: /   /   .   :   AM/PM   CHECK UP: YES   NO
CLINIC: COST:
REASON:
OUTCOME:
FOLLOW UP: YES   NO
FOLLOW UP DATE: /   /   .   :   AM/PM

DATE & TIME: /   /   .   :   AM/PM   CHECK UP: YES   NO
CLINIC: COST:
REASON:
OUTCOME:
FOLLOW UP: YES   NO
FOLLOW UP DATE: /   /   .   :   AM/PM

DATE & TIME: /   /   .   :   AM/PM   CHECK UP: YES   NO
CLINIC: COST:
REASON:
OUTCOME:
FOLLOW UP: YES   NO
FOLLOW UP DATE: /   /   .   :   AM/PM

DATE & TIME: /   /   .   :   AM/PM   CHECK UP: YES   NO
CLINIC: COST:
REASON:
OUTCOME:
FOLLOW UP: YES   NO
FOLLOW UP DATE: /   /   .   :   AM/PM

VET APPOINTMENT

DATE & TIME: /   /   .   :   AM/PM   CHECK UP: YES   NO

CLINIC: COST:

REASON:

OUTCOME:

FOLLOW UP: YES   NO

FOLLOW UP DATE: /   /   .   :   AM/PM

DATE & TIME: /   /   .   :   AM/PM   CHECK UP: YES   NO

CLINIC: COST:

REASON:

OUTCOME:

FOLLOW UP: YES   NO

FOLLOW UP DATE: /   /   .   :   AM/PM

DATE & TIME: /   /   .   :   AM/PM   CHECK UP: YES   NO

CLINIC: COST:

REASON:

OUTCOME:

FOLLOW UP: YES   NO

FOLLOW UP DATE: /   /   .   :   AM/PM

DATE & TIME: /   /   .   :   AM/PM   CHECK UP: YES   NO

CLINIC: COST:

REASON:

OUTCOME:

FOLLOW UP: YES   NO

FOLLOW UP DATE: /   /   .   :   AM/PM

DATE & TIME: /   /   .   :   AM/PM   CHECK UP: YES   NO

CLINIC: COST:

REASON:

OUTCOME:

FOLLOW UP: YES   NO

FOLLOW UP DATE: /   /   .   :   AM/PM

VET APPOINTMENT

DATE & TIME: /   /   .   :   AM/PM   CHECK UP: YES   NO

CLINIC: COST:

REASON:

OUTCOME:

FOLLOW UP: YES   NO

FOLLOW UP DATE: /   /   .   :   AM/PM

DATE & TIME: /   /   .   :   AM/PM   CHECK UP: YES   NO

CLINIC: COST:

REASON:

OUTCOME:

FOLLOW UP: YES   NO

FOLLOW UP DATE: /   /   .   :   AM/PM

DATE & TIME: /   /   .   :   AM/PM   CHECK UP: YES   NO

CLINIC: COST:

REASON:

OUTCOME:

FOLLOW UP: YES   NO

FOLLOW UP DATE: /   /   .   :   AM/PM

DATE & TIME: /   /   .   :   AM/PM   CHECK UP: YES   NO

CLINIC: COST:

REASON:

OUTCOME:

FOLLOW UP: YES   NO

FOLLOW UP DATE: /   /   .   :   AM/PM

DATE & TIME: /   /   .   :   AM/PM   CHECK UP: YES   NO

CLINIC: COST:

REASON:

OUTCOME:

FOLLOW UP: YES   NO

FOLLOW UP DATE: /   /   .   :   AM/PM

VET APPOINTMENT ✚

DATE & TIME: / / . : AM/PM CHECK UP: YES NO
CLINIC: COST:
REASON:
OUTCOME:
FOLLOW UP: YES NO
FOLLOW UP DATE: / / . : AM/PM

DATE & TIME: / / . : AM/PM CHECK UP: YES NO
CLINIC: COST:
REASON:
OUTCOME:
FOLLOW UP: YES NO
FOLLOW UP DATE: / / . : AM/PM

DATE & TIME: / / . : AM/PM CHECK UP: YES NO
CLINIC: COST:
REASON:
OUTCOME:
FOLLOW UP: YES NO
FOLLOW UP DATE: / / . : AM/PM

DATE & TIME: / / . : AM/PM CHECK UP: YES NO
CLINIC: COST:
REASON:
OUTCOME:
FOLLOW UP: YES NO
FOLLOW UP DATE: / / . : AM/PM

DATE & TIME: / / . : AM/PM CHECK UP: YES NO
CLINIC: COST:
REASON:
OUTCOME:
FOLLOW UP: YES NO
FOLLOW UP DATE: / / . : AM/PM

VET APPOINTMENT ✚

DATE & TIME:　　/　　/　　.　：　AM/PM　　CHECK UP:　YES　　NO
CLINIC:　　　　　　　　　　　　　　　　COST:
REASON:
OUTCOME:
FOLLOW UP:　YES　　NO
FOLLOW UP DATE:　　/　　/　　.　：　AM/PM

DATE & TIME:　　/　　/　　.　：　AM/PM　　CHECK UP:　YES　　NO
CLINIC:　　　　　　　　　　　　　　　　COST:
REASON:
OUTCOME:
FOLLOW UP:　YES　　NO
FOLLOW UP DATE:　　/　　/　　.　：　AM/PM

DATE & TIME:　　/　　/　　.　：　AM/PM　　CHECK UP:　YES　　NO
CLINIC:　　　　　　　　　　　　　　　　COST:
REASON:
OUTCOME:
FOLLOW UP:　YES　　NO
FOLLOW UP DATE:　　/　　/　　.　：　AM/PM

DATE & TIME:　　/　　/　　.　：　AM/PM　　CHECK UP:　YES　　NO
CLINIC:　　　　　　　　　　　　　　　　COST:
REASON:
OUTCOME:
FOLLOW UP:　YES　　NO
FOLLOW UP DATE:　　/　　/　　.　：　AM/PM

DATE & TIME:　　/　　/　　.　：　AM/PM　　CHECK UP:　YES　　NO
CLINIC:　　　　　　　　　　　　　　　　COST:
REASON:
OUTCOME:
FOLLOW UP:　YES　　NO
FOLLOW UP DATE:　　/　　/　　.　：　AM/PM

PET MEDICATION TRACKER

DATE	MEDICATION	FREQUENCY	DOSAGE

MEDICATION RECORDS

DATE	AGE	MEDICATION	GIVEN BY	NEXT DUE

VETERINARY CARE TRACKER

DATE	DESCRIPTION	LOCATION	AMOUNT

VACCINATION RECORDS

DATE	AGE	TYPE	GIVEN BY	NEXT DUE

PET VACCINATION CHART

YEAR:

PET NAME: DOB: GENDER:

DATE	VACCINATION	AGE	NOTES

WEIGHT TRACKER

DATE	WEIGHT	DATE	WEIGHT

WEEKLY PET JOURNAL W

WEEK OF:

MONDAY

TUESDAY

WEDNESDAY

THURSDAY

FRIDAY

SATURDAY

SUNDAY

NOTES

WEEKLY PET JOURNAL W

WEEK OF:

MONDAY	TUESDAY

WEDNESDAY	THURSDAY

FRIDAY	SATURDAY

SUNDAY	NOTES

WEEKLY PET JOURNAL W

WEEK OF:

MONDAY	TUESDAY

WEDNESDAY	THURSDAY

FRIDAY	SATURDAY

SUNDAY	NOTES

WEEKLY PET JOURNAL W

WEEK OF:

MONDAY

TUESDAY

WEDNESDAY

THURSDAY

FRIDAY

SATURDAY

SUNDAY

NOTES

WEEKLY PET JOURNAL W

WEEK OF:

MONDAY

TUESDAY

WEDNESDAY

THURSDAY

FRIDAY

SATURDAY

SUNDAY

NOTES

WEEKLY PET JOURNAL   W

WEEK OF:

MONDAY	TUESDAY

WEDNESDAY	THURSDAY

FRIDAY	SATURDAY

SUNDAY	NOTES

WEEKLY PET JOURNAL

WEEK OF:

MONDAY	TUESDAY

WEDNESDAY	THURSDAY

FRIDAY	SATURDAY

SUNDAY	NOTES

WEEKLY PET JOURNAL

W

WEEK OF:

MONDAY

TUESDAY

WEDNESDAY

THURSDAY

FRIDAY

SATURDAY

SUNDAY

NOTES

WEEKLY PET JOURNAL

W

WEEK OF:

| MONDAY | TUESDAY |

| WEDNESDAY | THURSDAY |

| FRIDAY | SATURDAY |

| SUNDAY | NOTES |

WEEKLY PET JOURNAL W

WEEK OF:

MONDAY	TUESDAY

WEDNESDAY	THURSDAY

FRIDAY	SATURDAY

SUNDAY	NOTES

WEEKLY PET JOURNAL   W

WEEK OF:

MONDAY	TUESDAY

WEDNESDAY	THURSDAY

FRIDAY	SATURDAY

SUNDAY	NOTES

WEEKLY PET JOURNAL   W

WEEK OF:

MONDAY	TUESDAY

WEDNESDAY	THURSDAY

FRIDAY	SATURDAY

SUNDAY	NOTES

WEEKLY PET JOURNAL

W

WEEK OF:

MONDAY

TUESDAY

WEDNESDAY

THURSDAY

FRIDAY

SATURDAY

SUNDAY

NOTES

WEEKLY PET JOURNAL W

WEEK OF:

MONDAY	TUESDAY

WEDNESDAY	THURSDAY

FRIDAY	SATURDAY

SUNDAY	NOTES

WEEKLY PET JOURNAL

W

WEEK OF:

MONDAY	TUESDAY

WEDNESDAY	THURSDAY

FRIDAY	SATURDAY

SUNDAY	NOTES

WEEKLY PET JOURNAL W

WEEK OF:

MONDAY	TUESDAY
WEDNESDAY	THURSDAY
FRIDAY	SATURDAY
SUNDAY	NOTES

WEEKLY PET JOURNAL W

WEEK OF:

MONDAY	TUESDAY

WEDNESDAY	THURSDAY

FRIDAY	SATURDAY

SUNDAY	NOTES

WEEKLY PET JOURNAL

W

WEEK OF:

MONDAY	TUESDAY

WEDNESDAY	THURSDAY

FRIDAY	SATURDAY

SUNDAY	NOTES

WEEKLY PET JOURNAL

WEEK OF:

MONDAY	TUESDAY

WEDNESDAY	THURSDAY

FRIDAY	SATURDAY

SUNDAY	NOTES

WEEKLY PET JOURNAL W

WEEK OF:

MONDAY

TUESDAY

WEDNESDAY

THURSDAY

FRIDAY

SATURDAY

SUNDAY

NOTES

WEEKLY PET JOURNAL

W

WEEK OF:

MONDAY	TUESDAY

WEDNESDAY	THURSDAY

FRIDAY	SATURDAY

SUNDAY	NOTES

WEEKLY PET JOURNAL W

WEEK OF:

MONDAY

TUESDAY

WEDNESDAY

THURSDAY

FRIDAY

SATURDAY

SUNDAY

NOTES

WEEKLY PET JOURNAL

W

WEEK OF:

MONDAY	TUESDAY

WEDNESDAY	THURSDAY

FRIDAY	SATURDAY

SUNDAY	NOTES

WEEKLY PET JOURNAL
W

WEEK OF:

MONDAY	TUESDAY

WEDNESDAY	THURSDAY

FRIDAY	SATURDAY

SUNDAY	NOTES

WEEKLY PET JOURNAL W

WEEK OF:

MONDAY	TUESDAY

WEDNESDAY	THURSDAY

FRIDAY	SATURDAY

SUNDAY	NOTES

WEEKLY PET JOURNAL

W

WEEK OF:

MONDAY	TUESDAY

WEDNESDAY	THURSDAY

FRIDAY	SATURDAY

SUNDAY	NOTES

WEEKLY PET JOURNAL

W

WEEK OF:

MONDAY	TUESDAY

WEDNESDAY	THURSDAY

FRIDAY	SATURDAY

SUNDAY	NOTES

WEEKLY PET JOURNAL

W

WEEK OF:

MONDAY	TUESDAY

WEDNESDAY	THURSDAY

FRIDAY	SATURDAY

SUNDAY	NOTES

WEEKLY PET JOURNAL

W

WEEK OF:

MONDAY	TUESDAY

WEDNESDAY	THURSDAY

FRIDAY	SATURDAY

SUNDAY	NOTES

WEEKLY PET JOURNAL W

WEEK OF:

MONDAY	TUESDAY

WEDNESDAY	THURSDAY

FRIDAY	SATURDAY

SUNDAY	NOTES

WEEKLY PET JOURNAL W

WEEK OF:

MONDAY	TUESDAY

WEDNESDAY	THURSDAY

FRIDAY	SATURDAY

SUNDAY	NOTES

WEEKLY PET JOURNAL W

WEEK OF:

MONDAY	TUESDAY

WEDNESDAY	THURSDAY

FRIDAY	SATURDAY

SUNDAY	NOTES

WEEKLY PET JOURNAL

WEEK OF:

MONDAY	TUESDAY

WEDNESDAY	THURSDAY

FRIDAY	SATURDAY

SUNDAY	NOTES

WEEKLY PET JOURNAL W

WEEK OF:

MONDAY	TUESDAY

WEDNESDAY	THURSDAY

FRIDAY	SATURDAY

SUNDAY	NOTES

WEEKLY PET JOURNAL W

WEEK OF:

MONDAY	TUESDAY

WEDNESDAY	THURSDAY

FRIDAY	SATURDAY

SUNDAY	NOTES

WEEKLY PET JOURNAL | W

WEEK OF:

MONDAY	TUESDAY

WEDNESDAY	THURSDAY

FRIDAY	SATURDAY

SUNDAY	NOTES

WEEKLY PET JOURNAL

W

WEEK OF:

MONDAY	TUESDAY

WEDNESDAY	THURSDAY

FRIDAY	SATURDAY

SUNDAY	NOTES

WEEKLY PET JOURNAL

W

WEEK OF:

MONDAY	TUESDAY

WEDNESDAY	THURSDAY

FRIDAY	SATURDAY

SUNDAY	NOTES

WEEKLY PET JOURNAL

W

WEEK OF:

MONDAY	TUESDAY

WEDNESDAY	THURSDAY

FRIDAY	SATURDAY

SUNDAY	NOTES

WEEKLY PET JOURNAL

W

WEEK OF:

MONDAY	TUESDAY

WEDNESDAY	THURSDAY

FRIDAY	SATURDAY

SUNDAY	NOTES

WEEKLY PET JOURNAL W

WEEK OF:

MONDAY	TUESDAY

WEDNESDAY	THURSDAY

FRIDAY	SATURDAY

SUNDAY	NOTES

WEEKLY PET JOURNAL   W

WEEK OF:

MONDAY	TUESDAY

WEDNESDAY	THURSDAY

FRIDAY	SATURDAY

SUNDAY	NOTES

WEEKLY PET JOURNAL

WEEK OF:

MONDAY

TUESDAY

WEDNESDAY

THURSDAY

FRIDAY

SATURDAY

SUNDAY

NOTES

WEEKLY PET JOURNAL W

WEEK OF:

MONDAY	TUESDAY

WEDNESDAY	THURSDAY

FRIDAY	SATURDAY

SUNDAY	NOTES

WEEKLY PET JOURNAL

W

WEEK OF:

MONDAY

TUESDAY

WEDNESDAY

THURSDAY

FRIDAY

SATURDAY

SUNDAY

NOTES

WEEKLY PET JOURNAL

W

WEEK OF:

MONDAY	TUESDAY

WEDNESDAY	THURSDAY

FRIDAY	SATURDAY

SUNDAY	NOTES

WEEKLY PET JOURNAL

W

WEEK OF:

MONDAY	TUESDAY

WEDNESDAY	THURSDAY

FRIDAY	SATURDAY

SUNDAY	NOTES

WEEKLY PET JOURNAL W

WEEK OF:

MONDAY	TUESDAY

WEDNESDAY	THURSDAY

FRIDAY	SATURDAY

SUNDAY	NOTES

WEEKLY PET JOURNAL   W

WEEK OF:

MONDAY	TUESDAY

WEDNESDAY	THURSDAY

FRIDAY	SATURDAY

SUNDAY	NOTES

WEEKLY PET JOURNAL   W

WEEK OF:

MONDAY	TUESDAY

WEDNESDAY	THURSDAY

FRIDAY	SATURDAY

SUNDAY	NOTES

WEEKLY PET JOURNAL   W

WEEK OF:

MONDAY	TUESDAY

WEDNESDAY	THURSDAY

FRIDAY	SATURDAY

SUNDAY	NOTES

WEEKLY PET JOURNAL

W

WEEK OF:

MONDAY

TUESDAY

WEDNESDAY

THURSDAY

FRIDAY

SATURDAY

SUNDAY

NOTES

JANUARY

FEBRUARY

MARCH

APRIL

MAY

JUNE

MONTHLY PET JOURNAL

M2

JULY

AUGUST

SEPTEMBER

OCTOBER

NOVEMBER

DECEMBER

PREVENTATIVE MEDICATION

FLEA&TICK

JANUARY	FEBRUARY	MARCH	APRIL

MAY	JUNE	JULY	AUGUST

SEPTEMBER	OCTOBER	NOVEMBER	DECEMBER

HEARTWORM

JANUARY	FEBRUARY	MARCH	APRIL

MAY	JUNE	JULY	AUGUST

SEPTEMBER	OCTOBER	NOVEMBER	DECEMBER

MY PET JOURNAL

MY PET JOURNAL

CPSIA information can be obtained
at www.ICGtesting.com
Printed in the USA
BVHW072318050721
611166BV00006B/395